Traditions Around The World
Musical Instruments

by Louise Tythacott

Traditions Around The World

Body Decoration

Costumes

Dance

Food

Games

Jewellery and Accessories

Masks

Musical Instruments

Series editor: Katie Roden

Designer: Loraine Hayes

Consultant: Anthony Shelton, Keeper of Non-Western Art and Anthropology, Royal Pavilion Art Gallery and Museums, Brighton, England.

First published in 1995 by Wayland (Publishers) Ltd
This paperback edition published in 2001 by Hodder Wayland, an imprint of Hodder Children's Books

© Hodder Wayland 1995

British Library Cataloguing in Publication Data

Tythacott, Louise
    Musical Instruments. - (Traditions Around The World Series)
    I. Title II. Series
    784.19

ISBN 0 7502 3832 1

Typeset by Loraine Hayes Design
Printed and bound in Italy by G. Canale C.S.p.A.

COVER: Three drums are played as part of a traditional dance on the island of Guadalcanal, one of the Soloman Islands in the South Pacific.

Picture acknowledgements:
The publishers wish to thank the following for providing the photographs for this book:
Bryan and Cherry Alexander 16, 18 (top); CEPHAS 44 (top, Howard Shearing); Bruce Coleman 36 (bottom, Jaroslav Poncar); Sue Cunningham 19, 27 (bottom); C.M. Dixon 16-17; Eye Ubiquitous *Cover* (James Davis), 9 (Jonathan Prangnell), 13 (Paul Thompson), 22-3 (John Miles), 25 (James Davis), 31 (James Davis), 33 (Thelma Sanders), 34, 35 (John Dakers), 37 (Julia Waterlow), 38-9 (Bennett Dean), 40-41 (James Davis), 44 (bottom, Matthew McKee); PHOTRI Inc. 26 (Aby), 27 (top), 29 (Peter Carmichael), 30; Tony Stone Worldwide 7 (David Hanson), 10-11 (Ken Welsh), 20 (top, David Hiser), 22 (Claudio Capone), 32 (Hilarie Kavanagh), 36 (top, Bushnell/Soifer), 43 (Suzanne and Nick Geary); Topham Picturepoint 11, 12, 14, 15 (both), 18 (bottom), 24, 38, 39, 41, 42; Wayland Picture Library 8, 10, 20 (bottom).
Artwork by Peter Bull.

Contents

▲ Arara children from the Xingu Basin, Brazil, playing natural bamboo pipes.

Berber girls from ▶ North Africa playing traditional stringed instruments.

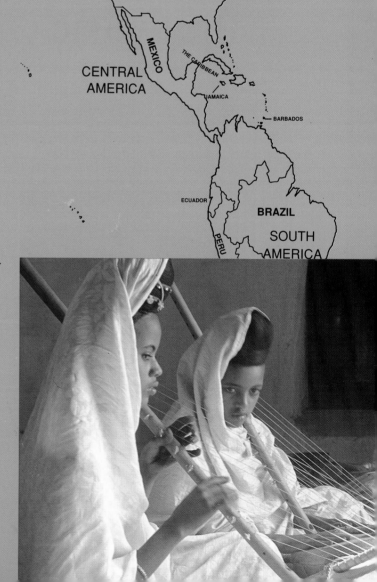

◄ Tibetan monks at a Cham ceremony. The same note can be sounded for several minutes on these trumpets.

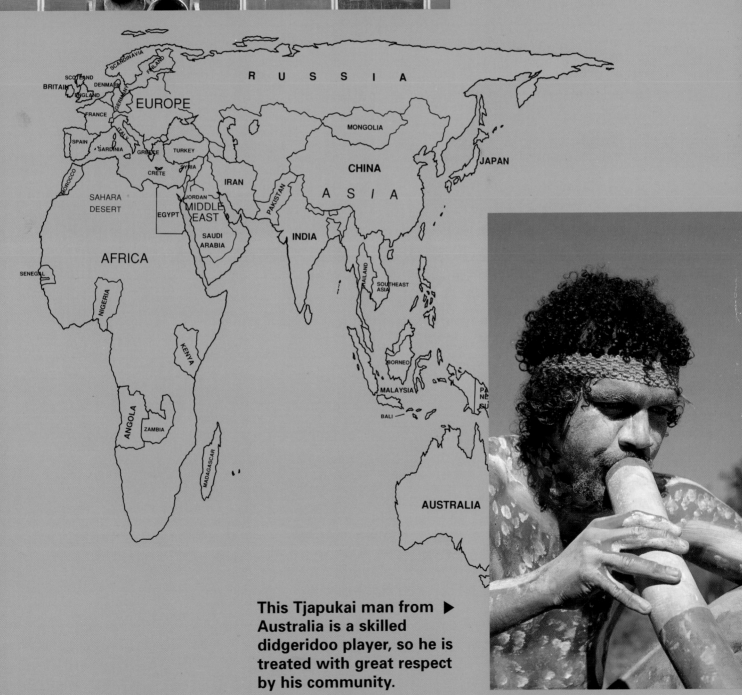

This Tjapukai man from ▶ Australia is a skilled didgeridoo player, so he is treated with great respect by his community.

5

Introduction

All human societies have created musical instruments in one form or another. The first instruments ever made were war or hunting trophies, and may have been used to imitate the sounds of nature. Shells, horns and thighbones have all been used to make music. Whistles made of reindeer toe-bones have been found which are around 42,000 years old.

Music is also a form of communication. In ancient times, music was used to speak to the spirit world, and today drums and rattles are still played in religious ceremonies. Instruments that are played to communicate with gods are sometimes seen as sacred. Animals are sacrificed to voodoo drums in Haiti, and offerings of fruit and flowers are given to the sacred gamelan orchestras of Indonesia (see pages 38-9). Musical instruments communicate not only with the spirit world, but also with humans. 'Talking drums' from Africa actually mimic the sounds of languages. Shell trumpets in the Pacific send signals, and church bells are often rung in Europe to tell people the time.

For centuries, the accordion, here being played in the Netherlands, has been used as a form of street entertainment in Europe. ▶

◀ One of the sons of a village chief calls people to dance by playing a tarpa, in Bapu Gaon, India.

▲ Music is used for celebration and the expression of feeling. These dancers in Zimbabwe are following a lively drum beat.

Many instruments are still made from natural materials. Animal skins, bones, tusks, beaks, claws, shells and hair are used, as well as stones, metals and woods. Nowadays, instruments can be made of modern materials like plastic, and of waste objects such as tin cans. Instruments can be highly decorated with feathers, bells and precious stones. In Africa, wooden instruments are carved by such skilled woodcarvers that some of them are treated as works of art.

Musical instruments around the world can make people dance, sing, love or fight; they are used to drive away evil, to heal, to charm, to communicate and to celebrate. Some instruments are so powerful that they are believed to cause thunder, earthquakes and rain. No society would be the same without its musical culture.

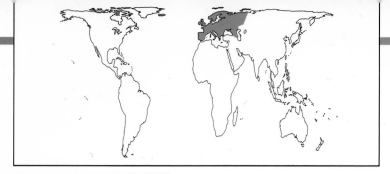

Europe

In many parts of Europe, modern electronic music has taken the place of traditional, hand-made instruments. Traditional instruments can still be heard at community festivals and in the home, but if, in the future, these instruments are no longer played, they will soon only be found in museums.

In the past, in the large town houses and courts of Europe, people played large musical instruments such as organs, harpsichords and pianos. Villagers in the countryside played smaller, more portable instruments such as the violin, tambourine, accordion and flute.

In Eastern Europe, groups of gypsies and Jews used to play to entertain people at weddings and other community festivals. Generally, the men played the violin and bagpipes, while the women played instruments such as the tambourine and jew's harp.

The tambourine is like a small drum, with a skin stretched over a circular wooden frame. Metal bells and discs are attached so that the tambourine jingles as it is moved. It is held in the hand and shaken, or the drum skin may be tapped with the fingers to create a rhythm.

A sixteenth-century spinet, an early form of piano. It was possibly made in Italy, and is built with cypress wood. ▼

◀ Spain is famous for guitar music. These musicians are performing at a festival in Malaga, on the Spanish coast.

▲ The gusle is used in Serbia to accompany a wide variety of folk songs.

The jew's harp is found not only in Europe but in many parts of the world. No one knows exactly why it is called a jew's harp, but the name has nothing to do with the Jewish people. It is a small instrument, made up of a thin, movable piece of metal fixed to a surrounding frame. The player plucks the metal with his or her fingers so that it vibrates in the mouth. The frame can be made of bamboo, wood, bone, ivory, iron or steel; metal frames produce a louder sound.

There are many instruments played in Europe that have come from other parts of the world.

The Spanish guitar, for example, is believed to have been introduced to Europe from North Africa. In Spain, this guitar is often played to accompany the energetic flamenco dance. Dancers play wooden castanets to beat out a rhythm in time with the guitar. Castanets originate from ancient finger-cymbals and are made from two round, wooden shells which are connected by a cord. The cord is then looped over the thumb. One castanet is called macho (male) and is held in the left hand. The other is called hembra (female), and is held in the right hand.

In Russia, wooden or metal spoons, called loshka, are played as musical instruments. These have long handles, to which small bells may be attached. The spoons are held between the fingers of the right hand and the two curved surfaces are banged together. Skilled musicians manage to use as many as four or five spoons at once. Sometimes a spoon is placed in the mouth and is struck with another spoon to produce different sounds.

The accordion is another popular instrument in Russia. There are various different types, named after the areas they come from. For example, the saratovskaya is named after the town of Saratov, where it was first made, and the livenskaya is made at Livna. The accordion is a hand-held instrument with a set of piano-like keys on one side, bellows in the middle and a set of buttons on the other side. It has straps which go over the player's shoulder, leaving his or her hands free to move the bellows and play the keys and buttons. It is also played in Ireland, where it is used to accompany jigs.

Bagpipes are used all over Europe. Traditionally, they were played in mountain regions such as those in Scotland, Spain and the Balkans, and they are also extremely popular in Poland and the Czech Republic. For each cultural region there are differences in the construction, sounds and playing methods of bagpipes.

Bagpipes always consist of a type of bellow – the 'bag' – that is moved in and out. Attached to this bag are pipes which the player blows down. The pipes create a low, continuous drone and the bag is placed under the arm so that it can be pumped in and out. Bags are often made of sheepskin and some pipes are decorated with beautifully carved, wooden goats' heads.

Scotland is well known for its traditional bagpipe music. Scottish pipes have a very distinctive sound. ▶

There are two types of Greek bagpipes, one played on the mainland and one on the islands of Greece. These pipes are from the island of Crete. ▶

In Brittany, a region of France, a simpler version of bagpipes, known as the biniou, is played for traditional dances and folk music performances. Polish bagpipes, known as koziol, are made of a whole kidskin and the pipe is decorated with a carved kid's head. Koziol slubny, or wedding bagpipes, were originally used for wedding celebrations. In Scotland, bagpipes have been played since the fifteenth century. In the early nineteenth century, they were played with violins to accompany country dances.

A far simpler wind instrument found in Europe is the whistle. Little clay whistles, made in the form of birds, are used from Russia all the way down to southern Europe. Whistles usually have one or two finger-holes, although some have none at all. The whistles with no holes are partly filled with water, and as the player's breath causes the water level to go up and down, the sound produced is like a bird's warble. The whistles with a single finger-hole sound like cuckoos. In Majorca, an island off the coast of Spain, pottery flutes used to be shaped like a man on horseback, but nowadays they show a man riding a motor scooter.

Another simple mouth-blown instrument is the conch-shell trumpet, used by fishermen to signal to each other. In parts of Portugal, a conch-shell trumpet is used to summon the local council and in north Wales, conch shells were traditionally used to call workers in from the fields at dusk.

Communication and signalling are important features of instruments in the isolated, rural areas of Europe. In the Swiss mountains, the music traditions are particularly distinctive. The alphorn is a long, wooden horn whose sound can echo throughout the Alps. It is used by herders to direct their animals. Similar instruments are used by herders in countries such as Norway, Sweden, Russia, Romania, France and Germany. Yodelling is another important form of communication in the Swiss Alps, because its sound can travel for many kilometres across the mountains.

▲ **The Swiss alphorn was originally used by herders to communicate with each other and to direct their animals.**

Mouth-blown instruments used to be important in rural areas of Europe for long-distance communication. Today, such instruments are usually played at folk festivals, like this one in Dubrovnik, Croatia. ▶

15

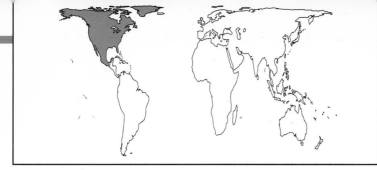

North America

For centuries, Native American peoples have used rattles, drums and flutes in their sacred ceremonies. Materials from the local environment were used, such as bones for flutes, animal skins for drums, and hooves, teeth, beaks and claws for rattles. However, when European settlers arrived in the Americas, from the sixteenth century onwards, they wiped out many Native American cultures. Many of the ancient musical instruments used by the Native Americans were completely lost, but some still survive today.

Drums were particularly important to the original peoples of North America, and were used in many of their ceremonies. Certain drums provided the rhythm for war dances and accompanied warriors on fighting expeditions. Some had decorations and rattles attached to them. These were known as medicine drums and were believed to have magical powers over the spirits. Small, hand-held drums were filled with pebbles, then sealed and used as rattles which were shaken over sick people to heal them.

A woman performs a traditional Native American song, accompanied by a drum, at a festival in New Mexico, USA. ▶

◀ **A rattle used by a Native American shaman to cure sick people. It is made from a dried tortoise.**

Today, the Iroquois people still use rattles as part of their healing ceremonies. The Iroquois have 'medicine societies' each of which has a different ritual associated with it. Their dances are believed to have healing powers. In the 'Common Face' dance, a singer shakes a turtle-shell rattle while 'Common Face' dancers dip their hands in embers, rub them together and blow ashes on the head, shoulder, elbows and knees of patients who wish to be cured. The singer may also bang a stick while singing. In recent years, the Iroquois have used rattles made from empty tin cans filled with stones.

Along the north-west coast of Canada, Native American peoples also use special rattles during healing ceremonies. Groups such as the Tsimshian and Tlingit shake beautiful wooden rattles which are elaborately carved into the shapes of animals and birds, such as the raven, which have religious significance. During celebrations, a shaman, or religious leader, wears an apron decorated with carved ivory or bone charms and deer claws. The charms bump against each other as the shaman performs an elaborate dance, creating a rhythmic, tinkling music. Drums are beaten and the raven rattles are shaken, to summon the spirits.

17

▲ An Inuit man of the Inuk people, playing a traditional drum as he sings. Only the rim of the drum is hit to produce a sound.

The Inuit people live in the Arctic areas around Alaska, northern Canada and the coast of Greenland. They live in small, isolated communities and have managed to retain many of their traditional musical customs. Song contests are particularly popular. Whenever the Netsilik people meet in winter on the flat ice, they hold drum dances together in a large, ceremonial igloo. The men make up songs and teach them to their wives. The women sing these songs while the men dance. Songs are very important to the Inuit peoples and are considered to be the property of the singer, who will teach them to other people in exchange for gifts. There are comic songs, dance songs, game songs, mimic songs, story songs, children's songs and personal spirit songs.

Many other peoples in North America have special songs as part of their musical traditions. The Amish still sing old tunes which no longer survive in Europe, and the many Jewish communities have music, songs and chants associated with worship.

From the seventeenth century to the present day, many immigrants have been arriving in North America from Europe. Often they have introduced their own musical instruments and cultures. For example, Irish immigrants brought ballads and dance tunes, including the reel, hornpipe, jig and set dance played on the violin, flute, tin whistle and bagpipes. Today, Portuguese music is still played in New England, USA, and Basque traditions from Spain can be found in Idaho.

Immigrant peoples have taken their own traditions to North America. These men in the USA are playing European folk music. ▼

In the southern USA, in places such as Kentucky and Alabama, an instrument similar to the French folk zither is still played to accompany songs, ballads and square dances. This instrument is known as the Appalachian dulcimer, named after the Appalachian mountain region where it is played. It is made up of a long sound-box of walnut or maple wood, which is placed across the knees. The strings are fixed horizontally across the box and are plucked with a plectrum, made from a turkey or goose feather cut to a long point and held in the right hand. The violin, which was taken to the USA from Britain, is also popular in this region and is often played to accompany jigs.

The arrival of African slaves had one of the strongest influences on North American music. In the seventeenth and eighteenth centuries, millions of African people were taken as slaves to the USA to work on the plantations in the south. They brought many of their own traditions with them, but were forbidden to play their drums. In Africa, drumming has always been used as a form of communication, and the plantation owners were frightened that if the slaves could send messages over long distances there would be a revolt. The slaves were only allowed to play stringed instruments; one of the most popular of these in the eighteenth century was a guitar-like instrument called a banja.

Originally, the banja was made from half a gourd on a stick, with a sheepskin nailed on. A similar instrument, known as a cora, is still found in Africa today. During the nineteenth century, the banja became popular with the white population, to whom it became known as the banjo. It was played in ballrooms to accompany singing and dancing. Today, the banjo is still played in the south-eastern USA.

A musician in Veracruz, Mexico, playing a drum and flute during a Volodores dance. This dance was also performed over 500 years ago, by the Aztec people. ▶

Jug bands developed among black American communities in the 1920s and 1930s. Generally, a jug was played by blowing across the top and was used as part of a string band. In rural districts in the southern USA, jugs continue to be used as folk instruments.

Sometimes, the jug is played with an instrument known as a washboard. This is an old-fashioned household washboard, which was popular as part of jazz groups in the 1920s. Normally, the player wears metal thimbles on his or her fingers, which are stroked rhythmically across the board to produce a very metallic sound.

Over 500 years ago in Mexico, the Aztec people played flutes made of terracotta and danced with dried butterfly cocoons filled with dried fruit attached to their ankles. Ceremonial rattles, called Chicahuaztli, were used by the Aztec and Maya peoples. When shaken, the rattles were said to make the sound of falling rain. Beautifully decorated versions of these are still played in Mexico by the Cora and Huichol peoples. Another instrument, a flute known as a chirima, which was originally used in Aztec times, is still played today in Mexico. The player inhales instead of blowing out, producing a sorrowful sound. The chirima is played at midnight from church towers.

◀ Mariachi bands are popular in Mexico. These folk bands stroll around town squares and market places, and people pay to listen to them.

Project: Rattle and drum

Rattles and drums are used in many Native American Indian ceremonies. Try to make your own rattle and drum.

You will need:
a yoghurt pot or any other plastic pot with a clip-on lid
Sellotape
a handful of small pebbles
a short stick

1. Take off the lid of the pot and place the pebbles inside.

2. Stick Sellotape around the lid to make it secure.

3. The pot can be used either as a rattle by shaking it rhythmically, or as a drum by beating the lid with the stick.

When the Spanish settlers arrived in Mexico in the seventeenth century they brought with them their own musical traditions and instruments, such as the guitar, which became popular throughout the country. Mexican mariachi bands are made up of guitar, violin and cornets players. Mariachis are strolling folk orchestras, composed of between three and twelve male musicians. Sometimes their singing is very lively, and at other times it is sad and sorrowful. Mariachi bands stroll around the main squares in many of the small towns in Mexico and stop to play for anyone who will pay. In the large city of Guadalajara, they can be found in the market places, where people go to listen to them or to hire them for dances and parties.

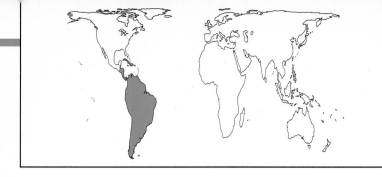

Central and South America

For thousands of years, the original peoples of Central and South America have played many different types of musical instruments. Today, reminders of their ancient past can be seen all over this region. Many different types of flutes, pipes and whistles are still used today in South America. Perhaps the most famous of all are the panpipes played in Bolivia, Ecuador and Peru. Among the Aymara people in Bolivia, panpipes are known as siku and are constructed from between seven and seventeen tubes of hollow reed, tied together in sets according to length. Sikus are played in orchestras; up to forty musicians can play in a group. In lowland South America, small flutes are made from animal bones. The shrill sounds that they make are believed to be the voices of ancestors.

The Maya people of Guatemala use large wooden rattles at the beginning of important religious festivals, to scare away evil spirits. These rattles can be up to 3 metres tall and are similar to the smaller, hand-held rattles used by football supporters in many countries. They make a harsh, growling noise.

Panpipes are played in many areas of Central and South America, and have been used for centuries. This man is playing a set of wooden pipes in Otavalo, Ecuador. ▶

▲ **Arara children of the Amazon rainforests in Brazil, playing pipes made from bamboo.**

Many of the musical traditions of Central and South America have been influenced by African cultures. In the seventeenth and eighteenth centuries, African people were taken across the Atlantic to the Caribbean, where they were forced to work as slaves on sugar and coffee plantations. Many Africans were also taken to Brazil, where their traditions were mixed with Amerindian, Spanish and Portuguese cultures to create many new instruments. Much Afro-Caribbean and Afro-Brazilian music uses drums, shakers, rattles and scrapers to create lively rhythms. Drums and rattles are particularly popular, and many different objects are used to make rhythmic sounds.

Scrap metal is used to make the drums played by steel bands in Trinidad, in the Caribbean. A large oil drum is cut down, leaving the domed top and part of the side. Concave metal panels are hammered into the top of the drum. They are hit with a rubber-tipped drumstick to make rich, metallic sounds. The drums are called pans, and there are five types – bass, cello, guitar, double-second and ping-pong. The deep, low sounds of the bass pan come from just three or four panels, whilst the ping-pong, which has the highest pitch, has about thirty-two panels. As there is no fixed pattern for the notes, the player must memorize the layout of the panels on each individual drum. It takes a great deal of skill and practice to play steel drums. When a large band plays together, the effect is rhythmic and lively. Steel bands are now popular at carnivals all around the world.

On the island of Cuba, two main types of drum are used: the conga and the bongo, which are both African in origin. The conga is a barrel drum with one end made of boards, strengthened with metal hoops. It has such a strong sound that it can be heard for many kilometres. The bongo consists of two conical drums, slightly different in size, which are joined together horizontally and held between the musician's knees. The player hits the drum with his or her fingers and palms.

Drumming is the most important sound on the neighbouring island of Haiti, and drums are played at almost every major event. Certain drums are named after members of the family, such as the mama drum (the largest), the father drum and the baby drum. Haitian drums of African origin are sometimes considered sacred objects and may even represent a god. The most sacred drum, the assoto, stands over 2 metres high. Traditionally, an assoto was made only with the wood of a special tree, cut at full moon. An animal had to be sacrificed to the drum before it could be used.

◀ These steel drums, made from large oil drums, are being played in a steel band on the Caribbean island of Trinidad.

Rattles and shakers are a popular element of Afro-Caribbean music. A pair of hand-held rattles, known as maracas, are shaken to accompany drumming. Traditionally, maracas are made of hollow gourds filled with dried seeds or pebbles. Nowadays, some are made of wood and filled with beads. Another rattle, the cabaca, (pronounced 'cabassa'), is also made from a gourd with strings of steel beads around the outside. The gourd, which is held by a handle, is turned backwards and forwards. As the steel beads move, a gravelly sound is produced. Animal jawbones may also be used as rattles. Usually, the bone is taken from an ass and the teeth are wired loosely in their sockets, sometimes with tiny bells attached. When the side of the jawbone is slapped with the open hand, all the teeth vibrate in their sockets.

▼Afro-Brazilian music is characterized by rhythmic shaking, banging and tapping. The music played by Samba bands, at festivals and carnivals, is always very lively and energetic.

▲ A musician playing a marimba in Guatemala.

The marimba, a Guatemalan xylophone, is also thought to have come from Africa. Xylophones consist of a set of wooden slabs which are hit with sticks. The marimba has gourds of different sizes placed underneath the slabs. The gourds act as sound boxes to amplify the sound as the slabs are struck. Large marimbas can have over 130 slabs, and several musicians are sometimes needed to play them.

Many instruments also show the influence of European culture. Harps, for example, were introduced by early settlers. Today, harps are often made by villagers in Ecuador and Peru, and are played at ceremonies and festivals.

▲ Harps are played at ceremonies in many regions of South America. This is a festival to celebrate Independence Day (28 July) in Lima, Peru.

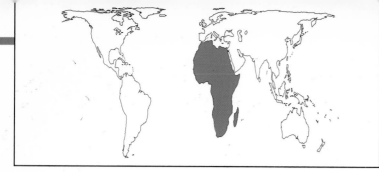

Africa

Musical instruments from Africa are very varied, ranging from simple-sounding instruments such as scrapers, drums, rattles and flutes, to more complicated ones like the xylophone and the harp. Music has an ancient history in Africa. Over 3,000 years ago, the ancient Egyptians played instruments such as the harp. In the fifteenth century, the people of the Benin civilization in West Africa played flutes and struck bronze or ivory bells to ward off evil spirits. This rich variety of instruments may still be found today.

Amongst the Berber peoples in Morocco, professional musicians travel in groups through the mountain villages during the summer months. The head of the group is the amdyaz, or poet, who announces news of world affairs. The amdyaz is accompanied by two drummers and a viola player, and by a clown who plays a drum or reed pipe to announce the presence of the group. Berber musicians may be heard at souks, or weekly markets, in Morocco, and they also play for weddings and family occasions in Egypt and other parts of North Africa.

These North African Berber girls are playing traditional stringed instruments. ▶

28

▲ These Tuareg nomads in Algeria are playing tambourines made from goatskin.

African drums are often highly decorated, such as the drums being played by these Chuka musicians from Kenya. ▶

Many African musical instruments are associated with religions and royalty. Long blasts of the Moroccan trumpet are used to signal the end of Ramadan, the Muslim period of fasting. In Christian Ethiopia, rattling metal discs, known as tsnasins, which are horse-shoe shaped, are presented to churches by government officials.

Drums are a very important feature of many African cultures. There is a vast range of sizes, shapes, sounds and melodies, and drums form an important means of expression. In West Africa, certain drums known as 'talking drums' are used to communicate over long distances. In countries such as Ghana and Nigeria, drum messages are conveyed over distances as great as 30 kilometres. They may be used to announce births, marriages and deaths, to welcome leaders or to communicate important information. The kalenga drum from Nigeria is famous for its

ability to 'talk'. By pressing the strings which run along the sides of the drum, the player can raise and lower the note produced, so that it sounds almost like a human voice.

The Asante people in Ghana have several talking drums. The main drum is atumpan, which only the chiefs may possess. It is made from a tree-trunk, which is cut down at a special ceremony. The covering is always made from elephants' ears.

African chiefs may use different names for different drums, which are inherited from generation to generation. Among the Yoruba people in Nigeria, all the different ancestors have their own drum music. The most important set of drums, or dundun, is called Iya-ili ('mother of drums').

A small, portable thumb piano is played in many parts of Africa. It is known as sansa in South Africa and Cameroon, and as mbira among the nomadic Masai people in Kenya. The thumb piano consists of long keys made of cane or metal, mounted on a wooden board. One end of each key can vibrate freely when it is plucked. The keys vary in length, and each makes a different sound. This small piano is held with both hands and the keys are plucked with the forefingers and thumbs, to make a twanging sound. Sometimes it is encased in a large gourd, which helps to amplify the sound.

◀ **Many African musical instruments have been taken around the world as people have moved from place to place. The cora may have been the origin of the banjo. This cora player is from Gambia.**

Xylophone orchestras exist in many regions in Africa. In East and West Africa, pit or ground xylophones are common. Wooden slabs are laid across the top of a pit, which acts as a sound-box. Among the Bantu peoples, xylophones often have a hollow gourd placed underneath the wooden bars. The gourd has small holes in its sides, covered with membranes made from the egg-cases of spiders. These membranes add a 'buzzing' sound when the xylophone is played.

Ground zithers are made by digging a small pit and stretching a string across it. As the string is plucked, the air in the pit vibrates and makes a noise. Other zithers have strings stretched across different types of sound-box, which are then plucked or beaten to make a sound. Tube zithers as well as ground zithers can be found in Africa. In Uganda, a stick zither known as tzetze is played. This consists of a stick to which a hollow gourd is fixed at the centre. A string is attached to each end of the stick. When the string is plucked, sound is produced in the gourd. Madagascar, off the south-east coast of Africa, is the home of the Valiha. This is made from a bamboo tube. Strings are cut from the outside of the tube and are left attached at both ends. Pieces of wood are inserted underneath the strings so that they vibrate when plucked. The player holds the tube upright or under an arm.

▲ **These women from Mauritania are playing a conical drum.**

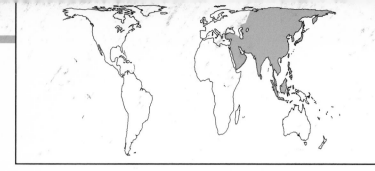

Asia

For centuries, gongs, chimes and bells have been used in religious ceremonies and performances all over Asia. Nowadays, they are still played throughout the continent.

Chinese musicians were probably the first to use these instruments, and the Chinese chime gongs are perhaps the oldest of all. The gongs hang from a wooden frame, in three rows of three, with a tenth gong suspended at the highest point In performances of Chinese Opera, important scenes are introduced by the irregular beating of gongs and bells. The music is timed to accompany the movements of the actors. Huge brass cymbals are clashed together, creating ear-splitting sounds, to indicate the bravery of warriors. In Cantonese opera there is a tradition that if the musician cracks or breaks the brass cymbals during the performance, a reward is given for his or her strength.

Bells are among the oldest ▶ instruments in the world, and there are many traditions surrounding them. These Tibetan people are sticking money on to a temple bell to bring good luck.

▲ **Gongs are believed to heal diseases and bring good fortune in some Asian cultures. This gong is being beaten during a festival in Japan.**

Many Asian instruments are used in religious rituals and ceremonies. In China and Japan, a wooden bell, known in Chinese as mu yu ('wooden fish'), is used to accompany religious chants. Mu yus are made of camphor wood, carved into the shape of a fish's mouth. Because fish never sleep, the mu yu is seen as a symbol of wakeful attention. The wood is decorated with intricate carvings and is sometimes painted red. Mu yus vary in size, from 5 cm to 75 cm across. They may be suspended, held by a handle or placed on a soft cushion inside temples. They are struck with heavy felt beaters.

In Tibet, musical instruments are often used in religious ceremonies. Perhaps the most remarkable instruments are those made from parts of the human body. The rkan-dung trumpet is made of a human thighbone covered with yak skin. It has a brass mouthpiece and may be decorated with corals or turquoises. The sacred rattle drum, called a damaru, is traditionally made of two human skulls. Cords or pellets are tied to the sides of the drum, which is turned rapidly from side to side to create a dry, rattling sound. The damaru, also called the monkey drum, is used widely, not just by priests and religious leaders but also by travellers in Tibet and snake charmers in India.

◀ **These Tibetan monks can sound the same note for several minutes on their long, ceremonial trumpets.**

Drums are widespread and very varied in Asia. They are an important element of Arabic music, which uses many different types. In Central Asia, the Kazakh people tie their kettle drums, or daulpaz, to their saddles and play them at war or when hunting. The Mongolian kettle drum, or kurga, was traditionally covered with the skin of a black bull. Because this animal was the symbol of power, the drum was used in warfare to co-ordinate battles. In Siberia, in northern Asia, drums are used in shamanic rituals to heal people. It is believed that the shaman can communicate with the spirit world through drumming.

The king of Myanmar (Burma) traditionally owned a set of royal drums. The set looked like a huge, tooth-edged crown, more than 1 metre high, glistening with gold and semi-precious stones. There would be an opening in the side of the set of drums to allow the player to enter. He or she would sit on a little bench, within the circle of drums. Only the player's head and shoulders

◀ **Drums are used all over Asia, in many different shapes and sizes. This musician from Ad Dila in Yemen carries his drum slung around his neck.**

▲ **Lusheng pipes being played at a festival in Guizhou, China.**

could be seen from the outside. The player would beat a set of up to 21 drums with his or her fingers and thumbs, and occasionally with a stick. The drums were arranged according to size, with the smallest on the right of the entrance and the largest on the left.

In the long history of Asian civilization, musical instruments have spread all over the continent, from one culture to the next. The Chinese lute, or pipa, originally may have come from Central Asia. Today, it is played in one form or another in Vietnam, Cambodia, Japan and Korea. In fact, many Korean instruments are identical to Chinese ones, because of the close historical links between these two cultures.

◄ **A sitar class in progress in Gujarat, India. The sitar is one of the most popular Indian instruments.**

The main instrument of a gamelan is the bonang, or gong chime. This consists of round gongs placed horizontally on a carved wooden frame. The musicians are seated as they play the bonang, and the gongs have a deep, majestic sound when struck.

In Java, gamelans are sacred and are believed to have supernatural powers. Incense and flowers are offered to them and there is a name-giving ceremony in

Indian civilization has also had a great influence in Asia, especially in the south, around the islands of Indonesia. In India, music is closely tied to religion and spirituality. It is believed to give people energy, develop emotions and courage, touch the heart and drive away evil. Special melodies, known as ragas, are believed to have magical powers and should be played only at certain times of the day. India has a great many musical instruments, ranging from elaborate horns to popular stringed instruments such as the vina and sitar.

Each of the many islands of Indonesia has its own musical style. The most haunting, magical music from this region comes from the gamelan. The gamelan is an orchestra composed of gongs, chimes, drums and enormous wooden or bamboo xylophones set in ornate wooden frames.

which the instruments are given titles, such as 'Rain of Scents' or 'Eternal as the Sea'. Some gamelans are so powerful that it is thought that their playing will cause rain to fall or human emotions to become uncontrollable. Other gamelans may only play at specific times. In the past, Indonesian rulers owned many gamelans to increase their power; great rulers on the island of Java had as many as 29 orchestras. Gamelan music accompanies the movements of the graceful dancers in Indonesian shadow plays. They may also play at gatherings, to welcome guests or to announce the approach or departure of the head of a royal family.

▲ The turbi is a wind instrument found throughout India. This man in New Delhi is using it to charm snakes.

◄ Gamelan instruments are often set in ornate frames made of wood.

39

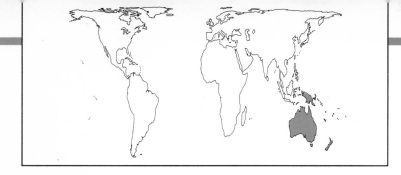

The Pacific

The islands of the Pacific are scattered over an enormous area. As a result, there are many varied cultures and musical traditions. The peoples of the Pacific have travelled widely over thousands of years, and some of their musical instruments have been passed from island to island.

Perhaps the most surprising instrument to be played in the region is a version of a Portuguese guitar known as a ukulele. A small guitar was brought to Hawaii by Portuguese workers in the 1870s. It became the favourite instrument of an officer who was nicknamed 'jumping flea' because he was so small. The Hawaiian word 'ukulele' means 'jumping flea', and this became the name of the instrument.

Shells are often made into instruments. In Samoa, the sound of the conch-shell trumpet was traditionally believed to represent the voice of the gods, and in Samoa and New Zealand, certain conch-shell trumpets were reserved for particular announcements relating to important families. In one village in Samoa, only members of the chief's family were allowed to make announcements using the conch. One Maori conch in New Zealand was so highly prized that it was blown only at the birth of the chief's first child.

This man from the Solomon ▶ Islands is beating the end of a bamboo pipe instrument during a celebration dance.

Nose flutes are common in the Pacific. In Fiji, they are made of beautifully decorated bamboo. Some have blowholes at each end and three fingerholes in the centre. The player blows with one nostril and blocks the other with his or her hand or a plug of tobacco. The Hawaiian bamboo nose flute, called ohe-hano-ihu, is used for serenading. The men of Siane, in the Eastern Highlands of Papua New Guinea, play 'sacred flutes'. They are played by pairs of men and are forbidden to women. The women are believed to have owned these flutes originally, but it is said that the men stole them and forbade the women to use them.

▼ The noble Vee'hala is said to be one of the few musicians able to play the nose flute in the Friendly Isles.

In northern Australia, ancient Aboriginal culture still survives today. Certain songs are considered sacred and music generally is used to teach people about their history and culture and about the worlds of nature and the supernatural. The most unique instrument played by the Aborigines is the didgeridoo. This is made of a long branch, which is buried in the ground so that termites eat a hole through the middle. The hollow tube is then dug up and is sometimes fitted with a mouthpiece of wood or clay. The player, who is always male, blows down the pipe, producing a low drone which is broken up by rhythmic patterns. The player vibrates his lips, and changes the sounds with skilful movements of the tongue and cheeks. The didgeridoo player is carefully picked from the local community and, once chosen, devotes the rest of his life to this profession.

Didgeridoos are played at Aboriginal corroborees – night-time ceremonies in which people gather around a camp fire to sing, dance and play instruments. The songman, who leads the ceremony, sings and beats time with rhythm sticks. Young boys dance, stamping their feet. Sometimes, boomerangs are clashed instead of sticks. In other ceremonies, the dancers strike the ground with bark pads attached to their hands, to create rhythmic noises.

◄ **Skilled didgeridoo players, such as this Tjapukai Aborigine from Queensland, Australia, are always greatly respected in their communities.**

▲ **Didgeridoos are highly prized instruments, and are therefore carefully decorated.**

Another Aboriginal instrument is the bullroarer, although this is also used widely in the Pacific and in parts of Africa. The bullroarer is an oblong piece of wood which is spun over the head on the end of a string. Small ones give a high-pitched noise, whilst the larger ones have a lower pitch. The speed of the rotation and the length of the string also affect the kind of whirring sound produced. In Australia, the Aborigines believe that the noise indicates the presence of spirits, and women are forbidden to approach when it is swung. In other parts of the Pacific, bullroarers are used to frighten away dangerous animals and to warn women to stay away from male-only ceremonies.

▲ **Drums are played by dancers during many ceremonies in Papua New Guinea.**

Drums are often used in Papua New Guinea to accompany dancing. Many drums have a handle at the left hand side, which the dancer can grip with his or her right hand. The skins of the drums are made of lizard or snake skins. For the Hevehe people in Papua New Guinea, the drum is the symbol of the dancer's power. Drum music is required for every stage of Hevehe dancing rituals, including preparing for the dance as well as during the dance itself. The dancer stops drumming only at the very end of the ceremony.

In Papua New Guinea, wooden drums are often intricately carved and painted. Slit-drums, known as garamut, are painted with a yellow dye called ochre, and the two ends are carved in the shape of crocodile heads, human figures or birds. Players strike the drum on one side of the slit, using the end of the beater rather than the side. As well as being used to accompany songs, such drums can also send messages to another village or to people beyond calling distance. On the island of Fiji, the lali is a slit-drum that was traditionally used to communicate all events with social significance, such as wars, victories, births and deaths. Each event was announced by its own rhythmic pattern. Nowadays, large lalis are used for calling people to gatherings or to church.

These Thursday Island dancers use brightly painted wooden drums as they dance. ▶

44

Project: Stamping tubes

On the Pacific island of Malaita, stamping tubes are used to accompany dances. They are usually made from ten rods of bamboo. If you cannot obtain bamboo, you can use pens or sticks.

You will need:
10 pens or small sticks that will not break easily
several large stones

1. Sit on the floor, and place the stones in front of you.

2. Place one stick between the big toe and the next toe of each of your feet.

3. Hold four sticks in each hand, between your fingers.

4. Grip the sticks firmly and beat out rhythms on the stones. If there is more than one person, you could work out rhythms that everyone can play together. Use the rattles you have made to accompany your rhythms.

In Malekula in the New Hebrides, the sound made by beating tall, standing slit-drums are believed to represent the voices of gods or spirits. Each drum is decorated with a human head or spirit head carved in wood above the slit. Because the drums are special, sacred objects, they are decorated with ornate carvings and paintings and are treated with a great deal of respect.

Whether they are used for communication, religious worship, or simply for entertainment, musical instruments are an important part of every culture of the world. Musical traditions have developed and changed over the centuries, but they are still as essential to every community and culture as they were in ancient times, and will continue to be so for centuries to come.

Glossary

Alps A mountain range on the borders of Switzerland, France and Italy.

Amerindians The original peoples of Central and South America.

Ancestors The people from whom somebody is descended.

Ballads Traditional songs that tell stories or poems.

Bamboo A tall, tree-like grass with a hollow stem.

Basque The culture and language of people who live in the Pyrenees mountain area of France and Spain.

Bellows An instrument with an air chamber that can be pushed in and out to create an airflow.

Boomerang A flat, curved piece of wood used by Australian Aborigines. When it is thrown, it returns to the thrower.

Camphor A strong-smelling wood with a sweet scent.

Cocoon A protective covering produced by silkworms and other insects.

Conical Having the shape of a cone.

Coral A yellow or pink, rock-like substance found in the sea, made from the bodies of tiny creatures, or polyps.

Cornet A brass instrument which is similar to a trumpet.

Drone A low, continuous sound.

Embers Glowing pieces of wood or coal in a dying fire.

Flamenco A traditional Spanish dance.

Gourd The skin of a large fruit that has been hollowed out and dried. Gourds may be used as dishes or bottles or to improve the sound of instruments.

Harp An instrument consisting of strings stretched over a frame, which are then plucked.

Harpsichord An early, piano-like, keyboard instrument.

Incense A substance that is burnt to produce a sweet, perfumed smell.

Inhale To draw breath into the lungs.

Inherit To be given the property of someone who dies.

Ivory The hard, white material which forms the tusks of elephants or walruses.

Jazz A musical form, with loose rhythms, which can be played individually or in groups.

Kidskin The skin of a young antelope or goat.

Lute A guitar-like, stringed instrument, with a pear-shaped body.

Maple A type of tree which is found in temperate climates.

Melody A sequence of musical notes which forms a tune.

Membrane A very thin sheet of material or skin.

Pellets Small, round balls.

Plantation A large estate or farm, usually in a hot country, where cotton, tobacco, sugar cane, coffee or other crops are grown.

Plectrum A small piece of wood or plastic used for plucking strings, often on a guitar.

Ramadan A Muslim period of fasting lasting one month, in which people are forbidden to eat or drink from dawn until dusk.

Shadow play A theatrical entertainment using puppets or actors whose shadows are projected on to a lighted screen.

Shaman A priest or healer who performs special rituals to heal people and to communicate with spirits.

Souk A market place in North Africa and the Middle East.

Termites Ant-like insects that eat wood.

Terracotta Brownish-red, baked clay.

Turquoise A greenish-blue gemstone.

Vina An Indian stringed instrument.

Warble A high pitched, vibrating noise.

Yak A Tibetan ox with long, shaggy hair.

Zither An instrument consisting of strings stretched over a sound box, which are then plucked.

Books to read

Seasonal Festivals series (Wayland)
Ardley, *Eyewitness Music* (Dorling Kindersley, 1989)
Sturman, *Creating Music around the World* (Longman, 1988)
Spence, *The Watts Book of Music* (Franklin Watts, 1993)
Introduction to Musical Instruments series (Children's Press, 1988)

Index

The musical intruments in this book come from many different peoples. Various types of instrument are listed in the index, such as 'drums' and 'percussion'. If you want to see how different musical instruments are used, look at entries such as 'festivals' and 'religions'. You can use the 'peoples' entry to look up musical instruments and traditions from the cultures mentioned in the book.